THE
FUNNIEST
RANGERS
QUOTES...
EVER!

Also available

The Funniest Liverpool Quotes... Ever!

The Funniest Chelsea Quotes... Ever!

The Funniest Spurs Quotes... Ever!

The Funniest Arsenal Quotes... Ever!

The Funniest Man City Quotes... Ever!

The Funniest Newcastle Quotes... Ever!

The Funniest United Quotes... Ever!

The Funniest Everton Quotes... Ever!

The Funniest Celtic Quotes... Ever!

THE FUNNIEST RANGERS QUOTES... EVER!

by Gordon Law

Printed in Europe and the USA.
ISBN: 9781696979054
Imprint: Independently published

Photos courtesy of: Igor Bulgarin/Shutterstock.com, CosminIftode/Shutterstock.com

Contents

Introduction...6

A Funny Old Game..9

Call the Manager...23

Best of Enemies...31

Game For a Laugh...39

Off the Pitch..49

Talking Balls...61

On the Booze..71

Managing Just Fine..79

Boardroom Banter..91

Player Power...97

Introduction

"When he first came to Ibrox he looked like Sacha Distel. Now he looks like Steve Martin." That's Ally McCoist's irreverent take on his old boss Walter Smith.

The manager famously led Rangers to their nine-in-a-row title success before returning to Ibrox to deliver further silverware.

Smith took no prisoners during both spells but showed he had a humorous side too, whether it was a sarcastic retort to the press or claiming McCoist had the "fattest backside in football".

Goal-machine McCoist is one of Scotland's biggest personalities who loves nothing better than to reel off a funny one-liner or to come out with a great anecdote to embarrass a fellow pro.

His teammate Paul Gascoigne was involved in many outrageous practical jokes and pranks, along with even more bonkers remarks.

Club legend Jim Baxter was another gifted footballer who kept fans entertained both on and off the pitch with his drinking exploits and hilarious sound bites.

Andy Goram was a larger-than-life character with some cracking quips, Fernando Ricksen uttered some crazy statements, while Davie Cooper also showed his sense of humour.

Many of their brilliant bloopers can be found in this unique collection of funny Rangers quotes and I hope you laugh as much reading this book as I did in compiling it.

Gordon Law

THE FUNNIEST RANGERS QUOTES... EVER!

A FUNNY OLD GAME

"The Italians are known for that, boss. Fowl play."
Ally McCoist after Graeme Souness told the story about an attempt to poison Trevor Francis' chicken meal

"He picked up a teapot and turned round and threw it off a wall, and it missed Jimmy Bell by about an inch! I was petrified, absolutely petrified."
Lee McCulloch on Walter Smith's dressing room rant after defeat to FBK Kaunas

"The songs didn't bother me. My English wasn't good enough for me to understand the words."
Rino Gattuso

"He waded in with the kind of challenge Jack the Ripper would have been proud of... and then he growled, 'If I get another chance, I'll break your leg'."

Davie Cooper playing against John Greig for the first time

"I think I'm a clean person – if I'm going to spit on someone, I'll spit right in their face."

Lorenzo Amoruso

"Even if Rangers were to offer me a new contract and a guaranteed place in the team, I would still want to leave. I hate the place."

Erik Bo Andersen

"I knew that it was time to retire when there were players beating me that I wouldn't have peed down in the past."

Jim Baxter

"I told them I didn't collect losers' medals and threw it away. I think a couple of kids fought over who would get it."

Graeme Souness after the 1989 Scottish Cup Final

"We had some new fitness videos delivered in the summer and they were all in Dutch. I couldn't believe it."

Lorenzo Amoruso

"People always say it's a shame someone as talented as Ryan Giggs, or George Best before him, never played in a World Cup or European Championship and I don't want my name to be added to that list."

Barry Ferguson... Really?

"I'll play for Rangers for as long as I can, then spend the rest of my life being depressed."

Ally McCoist

"There are some players in Scotland who are sick of the sight of me and I'm sick of the sight of them."

David Robertson after quitting for Leeds

"I went to Walter Smith and he asked, 'Do you like getting in the papers?' I thought for a moment and said, 'Not really'. And he said, 'Well, why do you do it?'"

Paul Gascoigne

"I only support two teams; Rangers, and whoever is playing Celtic."

Davie Cooper

"Even now when I'm asked for my autograph, I wonder if they were one of those who booed me."

Ally McCoist on the rough times during his first stint at the club

"I can barely sit at the breakfast table in the morning and watch the rest of the boys eating eggs, sausages and beans – I couldn't do that. In Holland we only have bread with either chocolate sprinkles, jam or cheese."

Arthur Numan

"Some people want me to return to the Scotland squad but it will never happen."

Andy Goram

"There was never any thought in my mind that I did not want to play for Scotland ever again."

Andy Goram the very next day

"I can promise everyone in Scotland that I will be a better player next year now that I know what to expect up here with respect to the pitches, opponents, the banter with supporters, which grounds have trains going past 10 feet away, and which grounds are overlooked by houses with people sitting in their windows drinking cups of tea."

Paul Gascoigne after winning Scotland Footballer of the Year award in 1995

"Funnily enough I ate some dodgy prawns, but I'd better not mention that to Roy Keane!"

Phil Bardsley suffers a bout of food poisoning while on loan from Man United

"I think Jock Wallace made me captain because I knew more verses of The Sash than he did."

Jimmy Nicholl

"I'm hoping to get back in the team, but they have been doing well, so it's a Catch 23 situation."

Ian Murray

"My preference is to see a doctor in France. Treatment carried out on me in Scotland is turning out to be of inferior quality."

Stephan Guivarc'h upsets the entire Scottish medical profession

"When he first came to Ibrox he looked like Sacha Distel. Now he looks like Steve Martin."

Ally McCoist on Walter Smith

"With all the years I spent at college I thought I would master the local language at Rangers. The only trouble was everyone spoke with a Scottish accent... there was nothing I could understand when people asked me questions. I tried my hardest to grasp the meaning of what they were saying but it proved impossible. In my first few days there I found it utterly depressing."

French defender Jean-Alain Boumsong

"I was the only British player to play 450 games and never get a red or yellow card. That could even be a world record for a defender. Speed is all I had. No one could run past me. I couldn't tackle a fish supper."

Eric Caldow

"Before we started in this league I thought we'd be playing against fat amateurs. But I've encountered many good, young players. Even if they don't quite have the qualities to make it, they're hard-working."

Dorin Goian on experiencing the Scottish third division

"Players were not allowed into the club kitchen but I regularly used to help the chef out. I would fry eggs and serve them up to the staff, instead of them doing it for me. They loved it."

Fernando Ricksen

"In Great Britain, they are nationalists. In general, Italians are a pain in the neck to them because they dress well, know how to eat well and drink with taste. We are the centre of their envy."

The Italian Lorenzo Amoruso on why he believes Rangers fans want Colin Hendry to be made skipper

"Don't mess with Walter Smith, that's for sure. I tried to keep out of Walter's way. Because I knew Walter would just invite you into the boot room and then probably boot you about the boot room! Keep out of Walter's way!"

Derek Ferguson admits he feared assistant manager Walter Smith

"It'll kill me when I'm no longer going out there to entertain the fans. That will be the saddest day ever. I'll have to find something else to replace that. Maybe I'll go the Richard Gere way and become a Tibetan monk and find religion."

Ally McCoist

THE FUNNIEST RANGERS QUOTES... EVER!

CALL THE MANAGER

"Ninety-five per cent of the time I'd come in after a game and give someone a hug but that's not such a good story. That's not going to get you a headline in the News of the World on a Sunday morning, is it?"

Graeme Souness

"The other players are perhaps less talented, certainly less talented because Barry is talented. Today on the pitch I had a captain who is less talented – I know that Gavin is less talented than Barry."

Paul Le Guen's talent show

"I've got a team of big-heads... My players have no idea about football. They want to look good in their red and white [away shirts]. I'm sick of it."
Dick Advocaat fumes with his players after a defeat at St Johnstone

"I am angry, I am disappointed, I'm embarrassed. Careless attitude, careless passing, not enough people wanting the ball, not enough people demanding the ball, not enough people going into dangerous areas... totally lacklustre."
Manager Ally McCoist is not a happy bunny after drawing with Berwick Rangers

"I can't say anything. I am annoyed I can't say anything. In every country and every democracy we can say what we want. But they are waiting for me."

Dick Advocaat to the media after two Rangers stars were sent off at Hearts

"We will go down and have a drink with the Celtic management team – but it might be an interesting cup of tea."

Walter Smith after a defeat to Celtic which had three Rangers players sent off

"I won't be fining players for getting sent off."

Graeme Souness after he was red-carded

"What do you mean by lion's den? It's a football pitch. It's the same size as the one we played on at Ibrox. It's 11 men vs 11 men. I've never known a fan to win a football match. A set of fans can make noise and make the atmosphere very interesting for everyone that we can all enjoy. But it is not a lion's den. A lion's den is if you jump over a cage and you've got four lions chasing you and you're fearing for your life."

Steven Gerrard when asked if his team was heading into the lion's den at Parkhead

"Tore [Andre Flo] has a groin strain and he's been playing with it."

Alex McLeish

"The idea was to get the ball in Lustig, block it, block Scott Brown who was making the triangle with the other centre halves and with this block we could have space to explore after regaining the possession on the other side. But we could not do it on this match because we were a little bit lower on the part – the moment I call the medium block."

Pedro Caixinha. Erm, the medium block?

"The Spanish police did what was natural to them. The Rangers fans did what came naturally to them and charged."

Jock Wallace on the 1972 Cup Winners' Cup Final pitch invasion

"You have to remember that we have our blue noses to go along with the orange shirts."

Dick Advocaat on the Rangers fans who wore a Dutch shirt during the 2002 Scottish Cup Final win over Aberdeen

"I was pleased with the way he played considering serial killers get better publicity than he has."

Walter Smith praises new loan signing El-Hadji Diouf

"No comment, lads – and that's off the record."

Ally McCoist to a group of reporters during a Rangers media ban

THE FUNNIEST RANGERS QUOTES... EVER!

BEST OF ENEMIES

"Did I hate Celtic when we played them? Yes, of course I did. I ran out of the tunnel detesting the sight of them and even now I hate it when I see Gers players cuddling Celtic players. For 90 minutes they need to hate. It means too much to too many people. Why hug someone you should be kicking the f*ck out of to win the league?"

Andy Goram

"Me and three pals used to jump a wall and play two-a-side on the pitch at Ibrox. I always made sure we shot towards the Celtic end, so I could pretend to score in front of them."

Alex MacDonald

"In football, a day is a decade and the game before is another history. But it's different in Old Firm matches – the fans love you if you play sh*te in other matches but great against Celtic."

Mikel Arteta

"Celtic could offer me all the money in the world, I'd never play for them."

Jorg Albertz

"I met up with them and I got four hours of absolute dog's abuse."

Graeme Murty on his father's Celtic family

"It angers me to see Rangers or Celtic fanatics getting all steamed up in the name of religion when most of them have never been near a church or a chapel in years."

Derek Johnstone

"I haven't had the chance to kick a Celtic player for many years."

Terry Butcher ahead of an Old Firm veterans' game

"For a while I did unite Celtic and Rangers fans. People in both camps hated me."

Mo Johnston

"No matter how much money was put in front of me, I would never sign for Celtic."

Nacho Novo

"I walked into the Celtic directors' lounge with my Rangers strip on. I went to the bar and had a double whisky 10 minutes before the game."

Paul Gascoigne on his first Old Firm match

"If I did that, it wouldn't be the penalty box I'd be in, it would be a wooden box!"

Kris Boyd is avoiding a transfer from Rangers to Celtic

"I am sure to get my usual great reception at Celtic. Maybe I will stand in the centre-circle this time to get the full applause."

Former Rangers star Alex Ferguson ahead of a trip to Parkhead

"You need the balls of a rhinoceros to play in an Old Firm game."

Ian Durrant

"If Celtic never won another game it would be a source of enormous rejoicing to me."

Rangers vice-chairman Donald Findlay

"My father-in-law is a Celtic fan. I know he shouts at me at the game saying things like, 'Fergie, you're a wee so-and-so!'."

Barry Ferguson

"It [green] is the colour of Celtic. From now on, no one will wear boots of that colour."

Pedro Caixinha

"That's their problem, although I cannot say I'm not enjoying what is happening to them at the moment."

Ally McCoist on Celtic's financial woes

THE FUNNIEST RANGERS QUOTES... EVER!

GAME FOR A LAUGH

"I got so excited before the game that I started to hyperventilate. They got me to breathe into a bread bag just to get me right again."
John Brown on his Old Firm debut

"They are a fantastic side, with great individual players, but the desire and the work rate got us over the winning line."
Winning line? Kevin Thomson after Rangers' 0-0 against Barcelona

"Celtic manager Davie Hay still has a fresh pair of legs up his sleeve."
John Greig

"He went on about being a man. I offered him the opportunity to have it out man-to-man after the game and he didn't want to know."

Ian Ferguson on a clash with Celtic's Paolo di Canio

"Hopefully this will get me back in the good books."

Paul Gascoigne wants to impress his girlfriend after his winner at Aberdeen

"A complete fluke."

Mark Walters on his goal direct from a corner against Celtic

Q: "What's your philosophy on penalties?"

A: "Save them."

Alan McGregor ahead of the CIS Cup Final shoot-out against Dundee United

"Jock Wallace told us in no uncertain terms that Celtic had scored two unlucky goals, so we had better go out there and score three bloody good ones."

Davie Cooper on beating Celtic 3-2

"I found it all quite funny, to be honest."

Peter Lovenkrands after Republic of Ireland fans mistakenly booed his Denmark teammate Peter Madsen

"Are you not ashamed to be on the same pitch as me?"

Jim Baxter on Scotland duty to England's Alan Ball in 1967

"This is the best night of my career – apart from missing the penalty."

Barry Ferguson eyes the positives after his side's UEFA Cup semi-final win

"Gordon and I have both bet Gazza that Gordon will score more goals than him. I was merely protecting my investment."

Ally McCoist explains why he let Gordon Durie take a penalty against Raith Rovers

"I was going to score an own goal, just to say I'd got a hat-trick at Wembley. Then Denis Law, who had played in the 9-3 game, told me that he would kill me if I did that."

Jim Baxter netted Scotland's goals in the 1962 win over England

"You do things that are strange when you score. Once against Celtic, I ran behind the goal and jumped into the arms of a superintendent who was wearing ribbons on his cap. As I'm jumping on him I'm thinking, 'What the f*ck am I doing?'"

Andy Goram

"It was harder to miss than to score. I was as surprised as anyone when the ball went over, but I can forget. I doubt if anyone else will, though."

Peter van Vossen misses an open goal against Celtic

"Peter van Vossen did his Marty Feldman impersonation."

Ally McCoist on the incident

"Everyone knows he is a crazy Celtic fan."

Lorenzo Amoruso after a spat with Ayr United's James Grady

"I felt their player needed sorting out."

Fernando Ricksen after he karate-kicked Aberdeen's Darren Young

"Ally was good enough to phone my wife and tell her that I wasn't too badly injured. I asked him what she said and his reply was, 'Trevor, she can't believe I'm not playing'."

Trevor Steven was stretchered off during an Old Firm clash

Journalist: "I'm from the Sun."

Paul Gascoigne: "I'm from the earth."

"In the Coca-Cola Cup Final against Hearts... I wasn't having the best of games, Archie [Knox] asked, 'Are you all right?' I said, 'No, the last time I felt like this I had a double whisky'. So I had one and scored two goals in the second half. It relaxes you."

Paul Gascoigne

"As I walked off the pitch, all I could see was my dad in the stand with his head in his hands."

Graeme Souness was sent off on his Rangers debut at Hibs in 1986

THE FUNNIEST RANGERS QUOTES... EVER!

OFF THE PITCH

"I was thrilled to be named the fifth best-looking sportsman in the world – until Ivan Lendl had finished above me."

Ally McCoist

"Gordon Durie says he went to Taylor Ferguson for his latest haircut. It's more like the work of Duncan Ferguson."

John Brown

"If you asked me the most accurate thing I've ever read about myself, I would have to say that the person who revealed I'm a Bon Jovi fan got me spot on."

Walter Smith

Police officer: "Mr McCoist, do you have a police record?"

Ian Durrant: "Walking on the Moon..."

From Ian Durrant's autobiography

"I don't like being on my own because you think a lot and I don't like to think a lot."

Paul Gascoigne

"We were not driven out. I left in a career move. I'm not a violent person, but if I got the person who did all this, I'd wring their neck."

Mark Hateley responds to rumours he quit because he had an affair with a pal's wife

"The football in Scotland is fantastic but life in Scotland, to me, is depressive... they say it's a beautiful country but I have yet to see it. In seven months here, I have not visited a shop and I have been to the Highlands once."

Dick Advocaat. "Scotland has a lot to offer – perhaps he should get out a bit more" was the response from the Scottish Tourist Board

"One guy stopped his car. He said, 'Just watch what you're doing up here, be careful mate'. I said, 'Cheers, mate'. He said, 'Because I'll slit yer effin throat'. The training didn't go too well that day."

Paul Gascoigne

"The 80s were a strange time for music. You went from Sid Vicious wanting to kick your b*llocks to Boy George wanting to kiss them."
Ally McCoist

"While you're all here, someone is round shagging all your wives."
Paul Gascoigne to reporters outside his girlfriend Sheryl's house

"The food in Scotland is similar to Germany – McDonald's burgers."
Jorg Albertz

"I don't want to offend any woman, but not many players could say they can go back home and really talk about football like they do with another man."

Brian Laudrup on his wife Mette

"When I said I had no regrets, I'd forgotten about that haircut and it has come back to haunt me on several occasions."

Trevor Steven

"I just shook hands with him. Imagine how many boobs that hand's touched."

Paul Gascoigne on meeting Sean Connery

"It would be hard to find another girl with a name like that."

Fernando Ricksen on why he got back with his girlfriend Graciela – her name is tattooed on his arm

"I studied English at school for three years but it's not the English they speak in Scotland. I had to learn a different language and even now Ian Durrant is still too difficult for me."

Jorg Albertz

"If it wasn't for Tracey, I'd be an 18-stone bricklayer playing for Penicuik Athletic."

Andy Goram on his wife

"Ladies and gentlemen of the jury... Oh, that was last week."

Ally McCoist at a fan event, a few days after police were called to an altercation outside a local pub

"Hear about the two cows in the field? One of them says to the other, 'Hear you've got that Paul Gascoigne disease'."

Paul Gascoigne

"I was guided towards Rangers by God and he has lifted me up since I got to the club."

Marvin Andrews

"I was having problems with ex-wife Graciela and we'd split up. I was on the prowl again. That night I was damn proud of myself – banging Jordan was one hell of an achievement."

Fernando Ricksen recalls a memorable night with Katie Price, which cost him a £25,000 club fine

"One day, I was a Raith Rovers player who couldnae pull the birds at the Cowdenbeath Palais. The next day I was in Glasgow and the girls were throwing themselves at me. I wasn't letting it go by."

Jim Baxter

"I was surrounded by a mountain of old-age pensioners, they are in bed by 11pm and start moaning and ringing the police."

Fernando Ricksen had a row with a neighbour after setting off fireworks in his garden at 5am

"I don't know what it is with me, wherever I go there always seems to be bloody trouble."

Fernando Ricksen

"I've been on that peach diet. I eat everything but peaches."

Paul Gascoigne

"I'm not the first guy to miss the birth of their kid."

Paul Gascoigne was drinking with teammates when son Regan was born

"I now know why Rod Stewart and Sean Connery don't stay in Scotland. You can't get any peace. We're sitting ducks."

Andy Goram

"My dad's great – he never asked for anything, apart from a house, a 740 BMW, a boat and a canny wage."

Paul Gascoigne

THE FUNNIEST RANGERS QUOTES... EVER!

TALKING BALLS

"You must allow enough time to savour something that is so fantastic. It is like a woman – the longer you wait for one, the more you appreciate it. Every four years is fine."

Lionel Charbonnier doesn't want a World Cup every two years

"In America, once you're famous they adore you for the rest of your life. Plus, the pina coladas are great."

Paul Gascoigne on a possible move to the US

"If I had to choose between cricket and football it would be cricket every time."

Andy Goram

"Bunion isn't afraid to put his head in where it hurts. And by the looks of him, he's proved that over and over again in his career."

Ally McCoist on Kilmarnock's Paul Wright

Q: "Who did you prefer playing for – Rangers or Celtic?"

A: "Spurs."

Alfie Conn

"I knew my England career was not going to get off the mark again when the manager Graham Taylor kept calling me Tony. That's my dad's name."

Mark Hateley

"They should be in the kitchen. I'm serious. That's where they should be.... Take them seriously? We might if they didn't look like the bouncers from Victoria's."

John Brown on women footballers

"They want to use me as a centre forward because I'd be the biggest player in the country."

The 5ft 9in Ian Durrant on a potential move to Japan

"When he was at Ibrox he crashed so many sponsors' cars he was eventually given a sponsor's dodgem."

Ally McCoist on Falkirk's David Hagen

"He's got more skill than I had at that age – or maybe even now."

Colin Hendry on his five-year-old son

"See the boy Rudyard Kipling, who said it wasn't whether you won or lost but how you played the game that mattered. Well, he obviously never played football. Winning is the only thing that matters."

Andy Goram gets Kipling mixed up with Grantland Rice

"A real player can always make a monkey out of a gorilla."

Jim Baxter

"The last time I saw something like that, it was crawling out of Sigourney Weaver's stomach."

Ally McCoist on Dundee United's David Bowman

"I don't know much about him, although I know that he played for Scotland. I think he scored five goals for the national side – so that pretty much says it all. I am 22 and have beaten that record at a professional level already. I read his quotes about me and I think he's a joke. Did he play for Celtic? I don't have a clue. I know pretty much all the top footballers and at first, I wondered if he was a cricketer. I had never even heard of him."

Kyle Lafferty on Charlie Nicholas

"The places he goes and the places I go probably differ, with the tan and the teeth and all that. They're not the type of establishments I rock up at – I'm not having a mid-life crisis!"

Joey Barton hasn't yet bumped into Celtic boss Brendan Rodgers

"I've always believed in treating the ball like a woman. Give it a cuddle, caress it a wee bit, take your time, and you'll get the desired response."

Jim Baxter

"His brother Wan is a better player."

Ally McCoist on Dylan Kerr

"It was football for men. You'd go in for the ball two-footed and then look to see whether your opponent could still stand up. I don't have a septum in my nose any more. It's all broken and covered in scars. My front teeth also got knocked out – I was elbowed countless times."

Fernando Ricksen on the physical nature of Scottish football

"I was really impressed [John Henry] scored a hat-trick against Morton in the fifth round – until I realised Brian Reid had been playing [in defence] for Morton."

Ally McCoist fires shots at his former teammate Brian Reid

"When Charlie Cooke sells you a dummy, you have to pay to get back in the ground."

Jim Baxter

"Scotland is not an international team – it's a mix of sheep shaggers."

Paul Gascoigne

"My mother came to watch me one day when I was about 13 years old. Later she told me, 'Don't try to copy your father. That's the worst thing you can do because I can't stand him [being] on the pitch!'."

Brian Laudrup

THE FUNNIEST RANGERS QUOTES... EVER!

ON THE BOOZE

"I didn't know Walter [Smith], but I knew he must be Scottish because I saw him carrying big discount cases of lager back from the supermarket."

Paul Gascoigne when he first met the manager in Florida

"That was exaggerated. Let's face it, tap water in Belarus isn't all that great. Do you really think I would drink a bloody flower vase of water?"

Fernando Ricksen allegedly got up to drunken mischief while he was on international duty with Holland

"Everyone thought Brian [Laudrup] was clean living. You should have seen him crawling along the hotel corridor, drunk, while on pre-season tour."

John Brown

"My hero's Bryan Robson. He's the only player I've ever known who could drink 16 pints and still play football the next day."

Paul Gascoigne

"All the great players I've ever known have enjoyed a good drink."

Jim Baxter

"I hear Big Fergie likes a few pints, loves to stay out late and chase the birds and gives a bit of lip in training; in my book he has all the ingredients of a good footballer."

Jim Baxter on Duncan Ferguson

"I can't dream up worse people to be in rehab together than Durrant, McCoist and big Norman Whiteside. It's like sending Oliver Reed and Dean Martin to the Betty Ford clinic together."

Ally McCoist

"You know if everything is going well, you get drunk for a couple of days."

Paul Gascoigne on life at Rangers

Don Revie: "I'm told you drink everything brewed and distilled around here, there aren't enough women for you to chase, and you're not averse to the odd brawl."

Jim Baxter: "Aye, you're very well informed."

"It's a miracle I have as many wines as this because Andy Goram came for a week last summer and he insisted on sleeping down here."

Brian Laudrup on the wine cellar at his Denmark home

"I took good care not to take to the field when I was drunk."

Fernando Ricksen

"One supporters' club 'do' I used to attend started on the Saturday night and we stayed all Sunday and got home on Monday. We called it the equestrian because it was a three-day event."

Andy Goram

"I sink a few bevvies on Saturday nights, and maybe one night early midweek. The rest of the week I stay home with my parents and watch television."

Jim Baxter

"The team that drinks together wins together."

Richard Gough

"The man with the safest hands in football, especially when there happens to be a white wine and soda clasped in them."

Ally McCoist on Andy Goram

"This reputation as a boozer bewilders me because he can't drink. Try taking him to TGI Friday's for cocktails and you're on a winner. It's a cheap night."

Ian Durrant on Paul Gascoigne

"I don't drink except when we win a trophy. People must think I'm an alcoholic."

Ian Ferguson after winning his 23rd Rangers medal

THE FUNNIEST RANGERS QUOTES... EVER!

MANAGING JUST FINE

"There was a story last week that I was leaving in 2002 and I had told my friends that. I don't know where it came from. I don't have that many friends."

Dick Advocaat

"That's a good try. It's a terrific try because we've already tried that before. He said, 'Do you want to talk about referees?' And I said, 'No'. Then you gradually tried to introduce it. It's a terrific try, but I'm still not answering it."

Walter Smith is not getting fooled by a reporter to comment about the SPL referees' strike

"The vampires taste the flavour of the blood and they want more, they need it. It's the same with the competitive teams and clubs, competitive players and competitive managers. They like the way the blood tastes."

Pedro Caixinha before the Betfred Cup semi-final with Motherwell

"There are too many hammer-throwers in the Scottish League. I sign a world-class player and have him put out of action after a game and a bit. This league is too tough."

Manager Graeme Souness after new boy Oleg Kuznetsov was injured

"When I was young, the boys used to call me elephant, because elephants have a great memory and I have a great memory."
Pedro Caixinha never forgets

"My greatest worry when I took over was that I might leave being the only Rangers manager never to have won a trophy."
Walter Smith

"We have beaten them 4-0, 4-1 and 4-2 but it looks to the press as if 6-2 is an even better score than the others. I totally disagree with that."
Maths is not Dick Advocaat's strong point

"I would love to be able to get to the stage where things here are all rosy in the garden. But I am not yet looking at pastures new, although right now we have given the critics a field day."

Alex McLeish is at one with nature after a Rangers defeat to Hibs

"Not at all. Irritation is not having bought the wife's Christmas present yet. That's a crisis in my books. I'll have that resolved this afternoon though."

Mark Warburton is asked if he was irritated by a swipe from Hibs boss Alan Stubbs

"Have you ever been to Las Vegas? What happens in Las Vegas stays in Las Vegas, so that's the first thing. I won't tell you what I don't want to [tell you], because that's private. Las Vegas is a great city but if you enjoy too much, what happens needs to stay there."

Pedro Caixinha on rumours of clear-the-air talks with the players

"You are trying to use me as a clown, and I'm not going to allow it. I feel like sometimes we live in a circus, and they want me to be the fish in the goldfish bowl."

Pedro Caixinha continues...

"People think he goes in and tells jokes with clown's feet and a rubber nose on, but he has a lot more to offer than that."

Alex McLeish wants to bring Scotland coach Ally McCoist back to Rangers

"We have scored 101 goals this season. Not bad considering we don't play with any strikers."

Walter Smith hits back at critics

"I always take my notebook into the toilet to sketch out some match situations."

Dick Advocaat

"I was brought up to only value the opinions of people for whom you have any iota of respect. Take from that what you will."

Mark Warburton responds to Chris Sutton who claimed the Rangers job is "too big" for him

"What I need to tell you, and it's a Portuguese saying, 'The dogs bark and the caravan keeps going'. That means that we are focused in our work. We are all together in the same direction."

Pedro Caixinha after a goalless draw with Hearts

"The only problem I have with players today is their music in the dressing room, which is just garbage."

Walter Smith

"I don't have BT Sport at home yet."

Pedro Caixinha is asked to respond to Neil Lennon's comments about him on BT Sport

"I knew it was time to go when I walked into the press conference and wondered if someone had died."

Walter Smith after the 1996 League Cup win

THE FUNNIEST RANGERS QUOTES... EVER!

"I have come to the conclusion that nice men don't make good football managers."

Graeme Souness

"As that great philosopher Doris Day said, 'Que Sera, Sera'."

Alex McLeish during a tough period

"I was nicely sacked."

Walter Smith on his first exit as manager

Q: Describe yourself in three words.

Steven Gerrard: "Miserable boring man."

The Rangers boss is only half joking

"He had the fattest backside in football at the time."

Walter Smith after Ally McCoist grabbed the winning goal in the 1993 League Cup Final

"I'm polite, I'm educated but I'm a f*cking tough guy."

Pedro Caixinha was criticised for giving the players a nine-day summer break

"It always gets back to the same question for me. Could a former electrician from Carmyle win the European Cup?"

Walter Smith

THE FUNNIEST RANGERS QUOTES... EVER!

BOARDROOM BANTER

"'Graeme, you're going now'. 'Walter, you need Durie'. 'Walter, you need McLaren'. These are the kind of strategic moves the chairman must make to ensure the smooth running of the club."

David Murray

"The Scottish Premier League threw us out. They then stole our money that was due for last year and are pursuing us to strip titles. It's like coming home, finding your wife in bed with the milkman, asking for a divorce and then a week later asking, 'Can you forgive me? We'll make up'."

Charles Green

"Take it, but make sure you put it back one day."

Bill Struth to fans who wanted to nab a piece of the Ibrox pitch

"That would be bad luck – to have the worst Rangers team in history and the worst chief executive in history at the same time."

Ally McCoist after Charles Green claimed the side was "the worst in Rangers' history"

"Complaints, moans, complaints. Now listen to this bit: 'And you can tell Walter Smith to get his finger out of his ar*e'. And ar*e is spelt A-R-S-S."

David Murray reads out a fan's letter to journalists

"His contempt and total lack of respect for my players, for our football club, for our support and Scottish football in general is appalling."
Ally McCoist on the return of former chief executive Charles Green to Ibrox

"He always tries to have a good relationship with his managers and if you're going to leave he always sacks you nicely."
Walter Smith on David Murray

"A few of us want to discuss super leagues but all the rest can talk about is the price of meat pies."
David Murray

"He was furious. His watch must have cost £20,000 and there were just six examples of it in the entire world. My first question was: 'How come it's not watertight?' He didn't find it funny. He'd had a phone and a credit card in his trunks as well."

Fernando Ricksen threw chairman John McClelland into a swimming pool

"There isn't anyone round the board at Ibrox who knows anything about football and that includes me. My knowledge you could carry in a mouse's handkerchief."

Charles Green

THE FUNNIEST RANGERS QUOTES... EVER!

PLAYER POWER

"He does look as if he can replace me. He's only got about 300 goals to go."
Ally McCoist on new boy Erik Bo Andersen scoring a brace on his debut

"I was welcomed to Ibrox by McCoist and Durrant spraying Ralgex all over my underpants."
Iain Ferguson

"The only way they differ is Andy is quieter on the pitch than Peter... and much louder off it."
Brian Laudrup compares clubmate Goram with international teammate Schmeichel

"His epitaph will read: 'Here lies Stuart McCall, a groundsman's nightmare. He made it into the Guinness Book of Records for the world's longest slide tackle – he dispossessed a guy playing on another park'."

Ally McCoist on Stuart McCall

"He is a very nice person. I know because he keeps on telling me."

Sebastian Rozental on Ally McCoist

"He's one of the most organised guys I know. He lives through a Filofax."

Trevor Steven on Paul Gascoigne

"If other humans could move their legs as fast as Spenny when he runs, the world 100m record would be about three seconds."

Ally McCoist on John Spencer

"I prefer to live one day as a lion, instead of 10 years like a rabbit."

Lorenzo Amoruso

"In training it was the English versus the Scots, Coisty came in our team because, as I told him at the time, he had played two games for the Sunderland reserves."

Terry Butcher on Ally McCoist

"These two boys are not the best of players, but at least they help make our team photo a bit more attractive."

Ian Durrant on Brian Reid and Derek McInnes

"He's a fantastic player. When he isn't drunk."

Brian Laudrup on Paul Gascoigne

Interviewer: "Would you like to be thought of as being as good as Rangers legends such as Paul Gascoigne or Brian Laudrup?"

Ronald de Boer: "Yes, they are probably at my level."

"I'd have backed Hateley. He had more time in the ring behind him."

Ian Durrant on a fight between Mark Hateley and Duncan Ferguson

"I couldn't be like him and he couldn't be like me. I can enjoy a Gazza joke but sometimes I'm glad I'm not married to him because he's talking all the time."

Brian Laudrup on Paul Gascoigne

"People have got this preconceived idea of me as a fat b*stard who can't move."

Andy Goram

"You can't live in Glasgow and be called Nigel. He's going to be Rab."

Ally McCoist to Nigel Spackman when he signed

"I don't make predictions and I never will."

Paul Gascoigne

"I don't like being called Kevin."

Kevin 'Ted' McMinn

"He's an intelligent boy who likes people to think he's stupid."

Ally McCoist on Paul Gascoigne

"He was furious when Lorenzo Amoruso was signed because he's better looking and his tan is real."

Ian Durrant on Derek McInnes

"And here is Ally McCoist to break me record and he does. I hate him."

Derek Johnstone observes the striker net his 133rd league goal for the club

"I have to say that I've never had any problems with Trevor's grip."

Gary Stevens on talk that Trevor Steven had a limp handshake

"I didn't understand why Gazza said he was taking his wallet on the pitch. Then he showed me a newspaper report where my mother said I would have been a footballer or a thief."
Marco Negri

"It was brilliant – he looked like Freddie Mercury."
Lee McCulloch on Kris Boyd's new tache

"This is not a man who looks like an athlete."
Ian Durrant on Andy Goram

"I just love him."
Jorg Albertz on Ally McCoist

THE FUNNIEST RANGERS QUOTES... EVER!

Printed in Great Britain
by Amazon